The Secrets of Baking with Olive Oil

by Maria Capdevielle

Text copyright © 2014 by Maria Capdevielle
Photography copyright © 2014 by iStock.com

All rights reserved. No part of this book may be reproduced in any form without written permission from the author.

The Secrets of Baking with Olive Oil 1
Introduction 5
About Olive Oil 6
Converting recipes to Olive Oil 8
The Sweet Pantry 10
Basic Recipes 14
   Pasta Frolla (Cookie Dough) 15
   Basic Pizza Dough 16
   Basic Focaccia Dough 17
   Basic Tomato Sauce 18
Cookies and Biscotti 19
   Lemon Rosemary Biscotti 20
   Pizzelle - Anise Waffle Cookies from Abruzzo 22
   Olive Oil Chocolate Chip Cookies 24
   Oatmeal and Raisins Cookies 26
   Chocolate Crinkles 28
   Black Chocolate Biscotti 30
   Chiacchiere - Crispy Carnival Strips 34
   35
   Taralucci al Vino - Wine Cookies 36
Cakes 37
   Lemon and Rosemary Olive Cake 38
   Capresa Cake - Chocolate Almond Cake from Capri 40
   Banana Bread 42
   Flourless Chocolate Cake 44
Sweets and Savory Tarts 45
   Crostata di Marmellata - Marmalade Tart 46
   Plum Tart 48
   Fiadoni di Pasqua - Savory Cheese Turnovers 49
   Sweet Tuscan Swiss Chard Crostata 51
Focaccia, Piadina and other Breads 53
   Sea Salt Focaccia 54
   Gorgonzola, Fig and Prosciutto Focaccia 55
   Potato and Parmesan Focaccia 56

Sun Dried Tomato and Feta Focaccia 57
Sage & Parmesan Focaccia 58
Cheese-stuffed Focaccia 59
Pizza Napoli.. 60
Pizza Margherita 61
Schiacciata d'Uva - Flatbread with Raisins and Grapes............... 62
Piadina with Prosciutto, Teleme Cheese and Arugula 64
.... 66
Piadina with Nutella... 67
Panzerotti - Fried Calzone with Cheese, Salami and Cherry tomato.. 68

Other Desserts and Pastries... 71
Cannoli Siciliani 72
Chocolate and Olive Oil Mousse 75
Profiteroles 76
Zeppole - Italian Donuts 78
Amaretto Truffles 80
Homemade Nutella (Chocolate Hazelnut Spread) 82

About the Author 84
About the Editor 84

Introduction

I grew up enjoying the flavor of extra virgin olive oil not only in salads, soups and other savory dishes, but also in biscotti, cakes and pastries. My mom would cook with whatever she had available, and, as in every Italian family, extra-virgin olive oil, was a staple of her cuisine. If a cake or cookie recipe called for butter and she didn't have any left, she would make it work with olive oil.

I was surprised to learn that almost no one in America bake with olive oil. Many chefs are afraid that the olive flavor will overpower the other ingredients in baked goods. They would be surprised to learn that extra-virgin olive oil is not only a healthier alternative to butter, margarine and other fats, but also gives a characteristic flavor and silky texture to cakes, cookies and other baked goods. In addition, the natural antioxidants in olive oil, such as vitamin E, help to keep baked goods fresh for longer periods of time compared to those baked with other oils or fats.

Olive oil offers a wide range of flavors that no other ingredient in the pastry kitchen can offer. There are more than 700 varieties of olives cultivated in the world. Each variety has a different flavor that can range from mild and buttery to spicy and peppery and anything in between. Olive oils from Northern Italy and France, for example, have a fruity peppery flavor while olive oils from Southern Central Italy, Greece, Spain and Turkey have a buttery rich flavor. The possibilities for chefs are unlimited and this is what I want to share with my readers!

In this book I am going to share to share some of my favorite recipes for cakes, cookies, tarts and breads along with the secrets of how to convert almost any recipe to olive oil. Because quality of olive oil is very important, especially for health benefits, I am also going to dedicate a chapter to choosing olive oil and storing it properly to get the best results.

About Olive Oil

There are four olive oil grades available in the market: extra-virgin olive oil, refined olive oil (light, extra light), olive oil (pure), and olive-pomace oil. The grades of olive oil are evaluated in sensory panels set mainly by IOC or USDA to determine the quality of the olive oil. Olive oils are tasted and evaluated for defect, percentage of oleic acid, and fruitiness. Generally speaking, the lower acid an olive oil is, and the less defects it has, the higher its quality.

Extra-virgin olive oil is the highest quality olive oil you can find in the market, and my preferred olive oil for cooking and baking. It is unrefined oil derived from the first cold pressing of olives and has less than 0.8 percent oleic acid and no defects. Although it is the most expensive olive oil, it gives the most delicate flavor to food and baked goods and contains most health benefits.

Refined olive oil is a blend of virgin and refined production oil, and must have an acidity level of no more than 1.5% acidity. It is less expensive than extra-virgin olive oil and I only use it for frying. I don't recommend it for cooking or baking because only extra-virgin olive oil provides the flavor and health benefits that I am looking for.

Pure olive oil and pomace oil are obtained using heat or solvents to aid extraction and not recommended for consumption.

When buying extra-virgin olive oil, keep in mind that olives are fruits. Because olive oil is a "fruit juice", it is best consumed fresh after extraction as is constantly oxidizing as a result of age, time, air and light exposure. For this reason, buy it in small quantities. Look for dark bottles that are displayed in cool areas away from heat and store them in the same way. Check for the harvest date on the bottle. It should not be more than 18 months. Since there is fraud in the olive oil industry, try to learn about the producers and their practices.

Like chocolate and wine, olive oil's flavor is not only determined by the way it is produced but also by the origin of the olives. Olive oils from Northern Italy and France have a fruity, peppery flavor while olive oils from southern areas of Italy, Greece, Spain and Turkey have a buttery, rich flavor. There is no single best olive oil; it is a matter of personal taste. Try different olive oils at farmers market and look for the flavor that most appeals to you. One of my favorite extra-virgin olive oils is Lucini from Italy. It has a rich, not too peppery flavor. I also like Raineri from Liguria. It has a buttery flavor. I have tried and like some of the Californian producers such as Olivina from Livermore, California Olive Ranch, and Corto. All of them produce outstanding olive oils at a reasonable price.

Converting recipes to Olive Oil

When I started researching for this book I soon realized that converting recipes to olive oil wasn't as simple as substituting the amount of fat that the recipe called for with olive oil. It was a matter of consistency and fat content.

Olive oil is about 99.9 % fat and its consistency is liquid. When a recipe calls for a liquid oil with the same percentage of fat as olive oil (for example canola oil or grapeseeds oil), you can replace it with the same amount of olive oil. You don't need to change the procedure.

The challenge arises when replacing olive oil with an ingredient that has a different consistency and a different fat content, like butter. Unlike olive oil, butter is solid and has less percentage of fat. Butter is made of approximately 80% fat and 20% water, lactose and salt. If a recipe calls for butter then you need to substitute 80 percent of its weight with olive oil. The other 20 % can be added or not as a liquid depending on the recipe and the results you want to obtain at the end.

For example, when baking American cookies (such as chocolate chip, oatmeal, etc), you do not need the additional 20% or the dough becomes too runny and the cookies don't hold their shape in the oven. The final outcome is on overly crispy cookie.

For shortbread, cakes, cupcakes and muffins however, the addition of 20 % liquid is beneficial. The kind of liquid to use (for example, milk, water or liquor), depends on the end result you want to obtain. Milk tenderizes, liquor or wine add flavor and water moistens the batter. Sometimes it may take several attempts to create the correct formula for your recipe. If the recipe calls for eggs, the best method is to mix the egg yolks with the added liquid and create an emulsion with the oil (like a mayonnaise). This mayonnaise has a similar consistency as softened butter and works wonderfully with shortbreads or butter cakes. After an emulsion is created you can add the rest of the ingredients.

If you want a lighter texture in your cakes, you can also incorporate more air into the batter by whisking the egg whites until foamy and folding in the batter at the end. For a more dense consistency in your baking product you can just add the egg whites without whisking them. As a general rule for cakes, all the ingredients should be at room temperature (including the emulsion you obtained with the egg yolks), and you shouldn't overmix your batter.

Shortbread is one exception. For these cookies it is better to have all the ingredients cold. The cold fat makes the cookies crispier.

Using this method you can transform almost any recipe to olive oil.

The Sweet Pantry

The recipes in this book are simple and you are probably familiar with most of the ingredients used. However, I encourage you to read this chapter before you start, to familiarize yourself with certain assumptions underlying the recipes and the use of ingredients.

Flour

All-purpose flour is used in most of the recipes unless otherwise stated. When the recipe calls for bread flour, it is because the final product is a yeasted bread (pizza, *focaccia* or sweet bread) and requires more structure than a cake or cookie. Bread flour has more protein than all-purpose flour. In bread making, it is important to knead the dough so the gluten from the protein is developed. It is the gluten from the protein that gives more elasticity to the dough, trapping the gases given off by the expanding yeast during the fermentation process. One of my favorite brands of flour is King Arthur and all my recipes have been tasted using this brand.

Yeast

Yeast is the leavening agent used in most Italian rustic and sweet breads. It generally comes in two forms: compressed cake or dry. I prefer to use dry yeast (or granular yeast) because it lasts longer than cake yeast (about 4 months in a dry place and up to a year in the fridge). It is sold in envelopes or in small jars, and comes in two forms: regular or quick rise. Quick rise yeast raises dough 50% faster than regular yeast. Although quick fermentation could be convenient for some bakers, there may be a loss of flavor and quality due to the rapid fermentation. For this reason, I prefer to use regular dry yeast in all my bread recipes. Activation of the yeast requires some liquid (milk, water, etc.) at the right temperature. For dry yeast, the right temperature is 110° F, and for cake yeast, it is between 90° F and 100° F. It is always wise to have a cook's thermometer on hand, as you can accidentally kill the yeast at 130° F or higher. When the yeast is activated, you can see bubbles on the surface of your liquid. This tells you that the yeast is working. If nothing happens at this point, it is because the temperature was too high (the yeast is dead), too low, or the yeast may be too old. At this point, try mixing in a tablespoon of sugar. If after 15 minutes, you still don't see any activity, it is better to start all over again with a new batch of yeast.

Eggs

All eggs should be Grade A Large. When the recipes require beating the egg whites in a bowl until peaks form, make sure that the bowl is totally clean and free of fat (including the fat from yolks), as fat will cut volume and prevent the peaks from forming.

Sugar

Regular granulated sugar is used in all recipes unless stated otherwise.

Milk

All recipes use whole milk unless otherwise stated.

Cream

"Cream" refers to heavy whipping cream in all the recipes in this book.

Ricotta

Ricotta is whole milk ricotta. It should have only three or four ingredients: milk, salt and a certain acid, or starter. In other words, if you can't pronounce the ingredients on the label don't buy it. Before using ricotta in your recipe, strain it overnight with cheesecloth, as the ricotta you find in the market usually has a lot of moisture in it.

Almonds

When a recipe calls for blanching the almonds, bring them to a boil in a pan with water, and then rinse them with cold water. The skins will come off as you rub the nuts between the palms of your hands. To get the best of the almonds' flavor, toast them in a preheated 350° F oven for 10 minutes. At this point, they should be used as soon as possible, as shelled nuts can easily turn rancid and stale. To grind almonds, use a nut grinder or a food processor. Be careful not to overgrind the nuts into a paste. To prevent this from happening, grind the nuts with a tablespoon of sugar, as the sugar absorbs the moisture from the nuts.

Hazelnuts

Toast hazelnuts in a preheated 350° F oven for 10 minutes. Rub them in a towel to remove most of the skin. Grind them following the same procedure for grinding almonds.

Basic Recipes

Although most of the recipes in this book are straightforward, there are some recipes that require more than one component. In this chapter, I have grouped all the building blocks for more complex recipes: *pasta frolla* (used for tarts and cookies), basic *pizza,* basic *focaccia* (used in several breads), and simple tomato sauce.

Pasta Frolla (Cookie Dough)

Makes one 10-inch tart

This recipe is adapted from Luca Montersino, an Italian pastry chef who specializes in allergy-free desserts. I use *pasta frolla* for cookies or for tart shells.

2 cups all-purpose flour

½ cup sugar

Pinch salt

Zest of one lemon, grated

½ cup extra-virgin olive oil

2 tablespoons water

3 egg yolks

Mix flour, sugar, salt and zest in a mixing bowl.

Pour the egg yolks and the water into a food processor. While processing, start pouring the olive oil in a thin stream and blend until it thickens into mayonnaise consistency. Add the liquid mixture to the flour mixture and mix with your hands or a food processor until you get a soft dough. Cover with plastic wrap and refrigerate for about 30 minutes before using. This dough keeps well in the refrigerator for a week.

Basic Pizza Dough
Makes 5 small or 2 large pizzas

I have more than ten different recipes for pizza dough. I particularly like this one because the addition of white wine improves the texture and flavor of the final dough. I use this dough not only for pizzas but also for *calzone* (baked pizza turnover), and *panzerotti* (fried pizza turnovers).

Sponge

1-teaspoon yeast

¼ cup plus 2 tablespoon water, warm (110°F)

⅓ cup bread flour

Final Dough

1½ cups bread flour

1 ½ teaspoon sea salt

½ cup white wine

¼ cup extra-virgin olive oil

Prepare a sponge: Mix yeast and warm water in a bowl and stir in the ½ cup flour. Let mixture sit at room temperature 30 minutes or until light, with tiny bubbles throughout.

In another bowl, mix the rest of the flour and salt. Set aside. When the sponge is ready, add the wine, the remaining flour mixture and the olive oil and knead the dough on a lightly floured surface for at least 5 minutes or until soft and elastic. Place dough in a large bowl, cover, and let rise in a warm place until doubled in size, (about 2 hours), or refrigerate dough and let rise overnight.

Punch down the dough and divide into portions (10 small or 6 medium pizzas). Shape dough into smooth balls and allow to rest at room temperature for about an hour before final shaping.

Basic Focaccia Dough

Makes ½ sheet pan

Focaccia is a specialty from the Italian region of Liguria. It is one of my favorite flavored breads. I like to serve it as an appetizer along with a plate of cheese and fresh fruits or as accompaniment to a meal. You can flavor this bread with almost anything. The most important thing is not to overcrowd the *focaccia*. It is best to choose no more than three topping ingredients for flavoring. I usually like to combine an herb with a seasonal vegetable or a fruit. In some cases I like to add a pairing cheese. This is my basic recipe for *focaccia* dough. I am going to share different variations of *focaccia* recipes in the bread section.

1 ¾ cup water

1 envelope active dry yeast

2 teaspoons salt

3 ½ cups bread flour

¼ cup extra-virgin olive oil, plus more for the pan

Warm ½ cup of water to 110° F. Dissolve the dry yeast into the water and let it rest for 5 minutes. Add the rest of the water and the flour, and mix until the dough comes together.

Add salt and olive oil and continue kneading until the dough becomes elastic (approximately 15 minutes). Put the dough into a lightly oiled bowl, cover with plastic wrap and allow to rest until it doubles in size (approximately 2 hours).

Basic Tomato Sauce
Makes 1 ¼ cups

1 (10-ounce) can peeled tomatoes, drained, preferably *San Marzano*

3 tablespoons extra-virgin olive oil

1 tablespoon minced fresh basil

1 ½ teaspoons fresh oregano, minced

1 ½ teaspoon garlic, minced

1-teaspoon salt

In a large mixing bowl, crush the tomatoes with the back of a wooden spoon or a fork. Add the olive oil, basil, oregano, garlic, and salt and mix well. Taste and adjust the seasoning with salt.

Cookies and Biscotti

Lemon Rosemary Biscotti
Makes 30 biscotti

I love *biscotti* in any form! They last for a long time and are great for dipping in your favorite drink. The rosemary and lemon zest gives a refreshing flavor to this version of biscotti. I like to serve them with a dessert liquor such as *Limoncello* or *Vin Santo*.

2 cups all-purpose flour

1 cup sugar

1 teaspoon baking soda

Pinch salt

1 egg

2 egg yolks

¼ cup plus 1 tablespoon extra-virgin olive oil

1 teaspoon vanilla

1 tablespoon lemon zest, freshly grated

2 tablespoon fresh rosemary, finely chopped

Sugar for decorating

Preheat the oven to 350° F. Line a sheet pan with parchment paper. In the bowl of an electric mixer, fitted with a paddle attachment, blend the flour, the sugar, the baking soda and the salt. In a small bowl, whisk together the whole egg, the yolk, the butter, the vanilla, the rosemary and the zest. Add the egg mixture to the flour mixture, beating everything together until combined. Divide the dough in half. Form each piece of dough into a log (approximately 2-inches wide and 12-inches long). Arrange the logs at least 3-inches apart on the sheet pan as they will expand in the oven. Brush the logs with water and sprinkle them with sugar. Bake the logs in the middle of the oven for 30 minutes. Let them cool for 10 minutes.

On a cutting board, cut the logs crosswise on the diagonal into ½-inch thick slices. Arrange the biscotti, cut sides down, on the baking sheet and bake them for 10 minutes on each side. Transfer the biscotti to racks to cool and store them in airtight containers.

Pizzelle - Anise Waffle Cookies from Abruzzo
Makes 2 dozen wafers

Pizzelle are also called *ferratelle*. This name comes from the heated iron ("*ferro*") used to cook them, but depending on the town where they are made, they are also called *nevole, ciarancelle, cancellette, catarrette*, etc. The original iron came with long handles to put it in the fire and it was usually engraved with the initials of the family it belonged to. Every family in Abruzzo had their own iron, and *pizzelli* were traditionally served at weddings to guests who kindly accepted them as a sign of good wishes and happiness for the young couple. Nowadays, they are served filled with grape marmalade, at almost any occasion.

2 cups all-purpose flour

1 teaspoon baking powder

1 teaspoon anise seeds

3 large eggs

Pinch of salt

½ cup sugar

1 tablespoon rum

⅓ cup plus 1 tablespoon extra-virgin olive oil

Zest of one lemon, freshly grated

Confectioners' sugar, for dusting

Mix flour, baking powder and anise seeds in a bowl and whisk to blend. In another bowl, whisk the eggs and salt until foamy, then gradually whisk in the sugar. When mixture is smooth, whisk in the rum, followed by the oil and lemon zest. Switch to a rubber spatula and fold in the dry ingredients. Let it rest in the refrigerator, covered with plastic wrap, for 1 hour. Preheat the *pizzelle* iron, and grease or spray it if suggested in the manufacturer's instructions. Using about 2 teaspoons of batter for each *pizzelle*, pour batter in the center of the iron, close, and bake about 1 minute. Then flip the iron over and cook the other side. Open the iron and if the wafer has a beautiful golden color, it is done.

Olive Oil Chocolate Chip Cookies
Makes 15-20 cookies

This is my favorite American cookie. This recipe was adapted from Classic Stars Dessert by Emily Luchetti to make it work with extra virgin olive oil. I reduced the amount of sugar because I found the recipe a little sweet for my taste.

2 ½ cup all-purpose flour

1 teaspoon salt

1 teaspoon baking soda

6 ounces plus 1 tablespoon extra-virgin olive oil

1 teaspoon vanilla extract

1 ½ cup brown sugar

2 eggs

2 ½ cups bittersweet chocolate, chopped in small pieces

Preheat the oven to 350° F.

Combine the flour, baking soda, and salt in a medium bowl and set aside.
Combine sugars, vanilla, and olive oil. Beat in the eggs one a time and mix after each addition until an emulsion forms. Gradually beat in the flour mixture. Add the chocolate pieces and mix until combined. Roll the dough into 1-inch balls with your hands and place on a parchment paper lined baking sheet 2-inches apart. You can also use a cookie scoop. Bake for 8-10 minutes, until lightly golden and set (mine took about 10 and a half minutes.). Allow to cool for a bit on the baking sheet, then move to a rack to finish cooling.

Oatmeal and Raisins Cookies

Makes 3 dozens

This is another wonderful American invention. This recipe is adapted from the Art of Simple Food by Alice Waters. I substituted the currants for the raisins.

½ cup raisins

¼ cup water

½ cup all-purpose flour

1 ½ cups (6 ounces) rolled oats, processed until ground

½ teaspoon salt

½ teaspoon ground cinnamon

1 teaspoon baking soda

3 ounces plus 1 tablespoon extra-virgin olive oil

1 teaspoon vanilla extract

¾ cup brown sugar

1 egg

Preheat the oven to 375°F.
 Put water and raisins into a saucepan. Warm over medium heat until the raisins are plumped and absorbed (10 minutes). Combine the flour, oatmeal, baking soda, and salt in a medium bowl and set aside.
 Combine sugars, vanilla, and olive oil. Beat in the egg and mix until combined. Gradually beat in the flour mixture. Drain the raisins and add them to the dough. Mix everything together until combined. Roll the dough into 1-inch balls with your hands and place on a parchment paper lined baking sheet 2-inches apart. You can also use a cookie scoop. Bake for 8-10 minutes, until lightly golden and set (mine took about 10 and a half minutes.). Allow to cool for a bit on the baking sheet, then move to a rack to finish cooling.

Chocolate Crinkles
Makes 3 dozens

These are the best chocolate cookies I have ever made, not only in flavor but also in presentation! With their contrasting black and white color from the chocolate and the powdered sugar, they will enhance any cookie tray. They require a little bit more work than other cookies, but I guarantee that it is totally worth it.

8 ounces bittersweet chocolate

3 tablespoons extra-virgin olive oil

Zest of one orange, freshly grated

1 ½ tablespoons brewed coffee

2 eggs at room temperature

¼ cup granulated sugar, plus more for coating the cookies

1 ½ cup pecans toasted

½ cup all-purpose flour

1 pinch salt

½ teaspoon baking powder

Powdered sugar for coating the cookies

Preheat the oven to 350°F. Ground the nuts in a food processor. Whisk the eggs with the sugar until the mixture is white and forms a ribbon. Melt the chocolate, the oil, the zest and the coffee in a bowl set over a pot with simmering water. Make sure the bowl is larger than the pot so it does not touch the water. Once the chocolate mixture is melted, remove the bowl from the pot and let it cool slightly. Mix in the egg mixture. The mixture will become thick as you stir it. Stir it just until combined. Mix together the flour, salt, baking powder and ground nuts. Stir this mixture into the chocolate batter. Refrigerate the chocolate mixture until firm (around 1-2 hours). Prepare two bowls, one with granulated sugar and the other one with powdered sugar. Roll the dough in 1-inch balls. Roll them in the sugar to coat them, then roll them in the powdered sugar. Place the cookies 1-inch apart on a baking pan lined with parchment paper. Bake them for 15 minutes. They should still be soft near the center but firm at the edges. Let them cool before taking them from the pan.

Black Chocolate Biscotti
Makes 5 dozen biscotti

Don't get discouraged by the amount of ingredients of this recipe. In my opinion, this is the best chocolate *biscotti* you can make.

4 ounces extra-virgin olive oil

6 ounces bittersweet chocolate, finely chopped

2 ½ cups all-purpose flour

¼ cup Dutch-process cocoa powder

1 teaspoon baking powder

½ teaspoon salt

¼ teaspoon baking soda

¼ cup Kahlúa

2 teaspoons espresso powder, dissolved in 1 teaspoon boiling water

1 teaspoon vanilla extract

3 large eggs

1 ½ cups granulated sugar

4.5 ounces milk chocolate, coarsely chopped

1 cup pistachios, coarsely chopped toasted

Egg wash with 1 yolk mixed with 3 tablespoons water

Preheat the oven to 350°F. Line two baking pans with parchment paper and set aside. Melt the chocolate and the oil in a bowl set over a pot with simmering water. Make sure the bowl is larger than the pot so it does not touch the water. Once the chocolate mixture is melted remove the bowl from the pot and let it cool slightly. Combine the flour, cocoa powder, baking powder, salt and baking soda in a medium bowl; whisk thoroughly and set aside. Mix the Kahlúa, dissolved espresso powder and vanilla in a small bowl. Set aside. In a large bowl beat eggs with electric mixture on medium speed for 2 minutes. Add sugar, in 3 additions, mixing for 20 seconds after each addition. Beat 1 minute longer. Reduce speed to medium low. Add Kahlúa mixture and chocolate oil mixture; mix thoroughly scraping down the sides of the bowl as necessary. On low speed, add dry ingredients, in 2 additions, mixing only to combine. Using rubber spatula, fold in chopped chocolate and nuts. Let batter stand for 10 minutes to thicken.

Portion the dough onto the baking pans, forming 4 logs, each measuring 1½-inches wide by 12-inches long, smoothing tops and sides with moistened hands. Brush tops and sides with egg wash. Bake for 20 to 22 minutes. Remove from oven and let stand for 20 minutes. Reduce oven temperature to 300°F. Carefully place one log at a time on a cutting board. Using a thin, sharp serrated knife cut into generous ½-inch slices. Lay slices on their sides and toast in oven for 12 minutes. Turn the slices over carefully and toast for 8 minutes longer. Allow cookies to cool on pans; the biscotti will become firm and crisp as they cool. Store biscotti, layered between sheets of waxed paper in an airtight container at room temperature for up to 3 weeks. If desired, biscotti may be frozen for up to 3 months

Chiacchiere - Crispy Carnival Strips
Makes 50 cookies

Also known as *cenci* in Tuscany, *bugie* in Piedmont, *sfrappole* in Emilia-Romagn and *galani* in Venice. *Chiacchiere* are the most popular *Carnevale* pastry in Italy. They are easy to make and fun to eat. Although their flavor is simple, the crunchiness of the dough makes this pastry totally addictive. The key to obtaining crunchy and light fried pastries is to heat the oil to 360°F.

1 ¾ cups all-purpose flour

2 eggs

4 tablespoons extra-virgin olive oil

¾ cup sugar

Zest of one lemon, freshly grated

P of salt

¼ cup rum

1 tablespoon vinegar

Confectioners' sugar for dusting

Canola oil for frying

Mix all the ingredients together and knead this dough for about 10 minutes until it is smooth and elastic. Let it rest for 1 hour, covered with plastic wrap. At this point, you can roll out the dough with a rolling pin to ⅛-inch thick, but the easiest option is to use a pasta rolling machine, starting at the widest setting and progressively decreasing to a setting of 3 out of 7. With a knife or a pasta cutter, cut the strips into rectangular pieces 4-inches long and 1 ½-inches wide. Heat 6-inches of canola oil to 360°F. Fry a few strips at a time, until golden (it should take 3 to 5 minutes per piece, otherwise raise or reduce heat) and drain them on paper towels.

When you dip the strips in oil, try to make them curl a bit on themselves so they form interesting shapes. Dust them with confectioners' sugar.

They're best eaten when still warm, as with anything deep-fried, but they can keep for one day in an airtight container.

Taralucci al Vino - Wine Cookies

Makes 100 cookies

These cookies are made to celebrate the grape harvest in Italy. Although they are very simple and easy to put together, they are complex in flavour and tasty. You can serve them at the end of a meal or as a snack with any wine you like.

2 ½ cups all-purpose flour

¾ cup sugar

1 teaspoon baking powder

Pinch of salt

¾ cup dry red wine

¼ cup extra-virgin olive oil

1 teaspoon anise seeds

1 lemon zest, freshly grated

Sugar for dredging

Preheat the oven to 350°F. Combine the flour, sugar, baking powder and salt. Add the rest of the ingredients and mix until you obtain a dough that is stiff, but fairly soft. Form the dough into a ball, place in a bowl and cover it with plastic wrap. Let it rest in the refrigerator for half an hour. Cut the dough into 1½-inch pieces that you can roll into 3-inches logs and then shape into rings. Dredge the cookies in granulated sugar and put them on a baking sheet lined with parchment paper. Bake them until they are light golden brown (around 25 minutes). Cool them on a rack and serve them at room temperature with a glass of wine.

Cakes

Lemon and Rosemary Olive Cake

Makes 8 servings

This is a fragrant and moist cake. I like to serve it with lemon sorbet or a lemon flavored whipped cream.

1 ½ cups all-purpose flour

1 teaspoon baking powder

1 teaspoon baking soda

Pinch of salt

1 cup sugar

Zest of one lemon, freshly grated

1 tablespoon fresh rosemary, finely chopped

½ cup plain whole milk yogurt

3 large eggs

1 teaspoon rum

½ cup extra-virgin olive oil

Center a rack in the oven and preheat the oven to 350 °F. Oil and line an 8 ½ x 4 ½-inch loaf pan with parchment paper and set aside. Whisk together the flour, baking powder, baking soda and salt.
Put the sugar, zest and rosemary in a medium bowl and rub the ingredients together until the sugar is fragrant. Whisk in the yogurt, eggs, rosemary and rum. When the mixture is well blended, gently whisk in the dry ingredients. Switch to a spatula and fold in the oil. The batter will be thick and shiny. Scrape it into the pan and smooth the top.
Bake the cake for 50 to 55 minutes, or until it is golden and starts to come away from the sides of the pan; a knife inserted into the center of the cake will come out clean. Cool on a rack for 5 minutes, then run a knife between the cake and the sides of the pan. Unmold and cool to room temperature, right side up.
Storing: You can keep the cake at room temperature for at least days or freeze it for up to 2 months.

Capresa Cake - Chocolate Almond Cake from Capri

Makes one (9-inch) cake, about 12 servings

This is a traditional almond chocolate cake from Capri. The original recipe calls for 6 ounces of butter. I substitute the butter amount with 4.5 ounces of extra virgin olive oil and 1.5 ounces of coffee for flavor.

4.5 ounces extra-virgin olive oil

8 ounces bittersweet chocolate

1 ¼ cup sugar

6 large eggs

1 ½ cups (about 5-6 ounces) ground almonds

1 tablespoon cocoa powder

Cocoa powder, for finishing

Set rack in the middle of oven and preheat to 350° F. Oil a 9-inch round cake pan and line with a disk of parchment paper. Set a large heatproof bowl over a pan of simmering water to create a double boiler. Put the chocolate into the bowl to melt, whisking occasionally. Add olive oil and mix to combine. Let it cool.

In the bowl of an electric mixer fitted with the paddle attachment, beat together the eggs and the sugars until light and creamy, about 5 minutes. Stop the mixer and add the chocolate mixture beating again until the mixture is smooth. Turn the mixer off and use a large rubber spatula to stir in the almonds and cocoa powder.

Scrape the batter into the prepared pan and smooth the top. Bake the cake until it is firm, about 35-40 minutes, or until an inserted toothpick or knife comes out clean. Let it cool before removing the cake from the pan.

Invert the cake to a rack and remove the pan. If the cake sinks slightly in the center as it cools, trim away the sides before inverting the cake to a platter.

Dust the cake with cocoa powder before serving.

Banana Bread
Makes one loaf

6 ounces extra virgin-olive oil

½ cup dark brown sugar

½ cup sugar

3 eggs

3 very ripe bananas, mashed

2 ounces rum

2 cups all-purpose flour

1 ½ teaspoon baking powder

½ teaspoon baking soda

½ teaspoon salt

½ cup walnuts, coarsely chopped

Heat oven to 325°. Oil and line a 6-cup loaf pan with parchment. Mix oil and sugar together in a large bowl. Add eggs, bananas and rum, mixing until almost smooth. Mix the flour, baking powder, baking soda and salt together. Working in batches, add the flour mixture to the banana mixture. Mix in walnuts and raisins. Pour in pan. Bake until firm on top or until an inserted toothpick comes out dry and clean (about 70 minutes). Turn onto a wire rack and cool before serving

Flourless Chocolate Cake

Makes one 9-inch cake pan

Chocolate and olive oil pair beautifully in this cake. You won't miss the butter)

8 ounces bittersweet chocolate, cut in small pieces

6 ounces extra-virgin olive oil, plus extra for the pan

6 eggs, at room temperature

1 cup brown sugar

1 tablespoon coffee

1 tablespoon brandy

¼ teaspoon salt

Center a rack in the oven and preheat the oven to 350°F. Oil a 9-inch round cake pan and line with a disk of parchment paper. Set a large heatproof bowl over a pan of simmering water to create a double boiler. Put the chocolate into the bowl to melt, whisking occasionally. Add olive oil and mix to combine. Let it cool.

Whisk eggs with brown sugar until the mixture is thick and forms ribbons when the whisk is lifted from the bowl and all the sugar has dissolved, about 10 minutes.

Add coffee and brandy. Fold the egg mixture into the melted chocolate. Pour the batter into the prepared baking pan, smooth the top and bake for 35 to 40 minutes. It is normal to see cracks on top of the cake as it cooks. Let the cake cool completely before taking it out of the pan. Serve at room temperature dusted with powdered sugar.

Sweets and Savory Tarts

Crostata di Marmellata - Marmalade Tart
Makes one 10-inch tart

This tart can be made with any kind of marmalade. I like to use seasonal fruits and make my own marmalade for this tart. Basically, the only thing you have to do is cook the fruit over low heat until it is very soft, add as much sugar as you like, and continue cooking until you obtain a very dense mixture.

Extra-virgin olive oil to oil the pan

1 *pasta frolla* dough recipe (page 15)

2 cups marmalade of your choice

Milk, for brushing

Center a rack in the oven and preheat the oven to 350°F. Oil a 10-inch round removable-bottomed tart pan with olive oil. On a floured surface, roll out the dough to a 12-inch circle about ¼-inch thick. Place the dough in the tart pan, pressing it gently around the sides.

Trim the excess pastry, and reserve the trimmings. Spread the marmalade inside the tart base. Roll out the pastry trimmings and cut into 1-inch wide strips. Lay the strips over the tart in a lattice pattern. Brush with a little milk, then bake in the oven for 20 to 30 minutes or until the pastry is a light golden color. Cool completely before serving.

Plum Tart

Makes one 10-inch tart

1 *pasta frolla* dough recipe (page 15)

4 cups purple plums, pitted and quartered

1 cup sugar, divided

2 eggs

1 teaspoon almond extract

½ cup ground almonds, blanched and pulverized in food processor

1 teaspoon baking powder

Preheat the oven to 375° F. Oil and line a 9-inch tart pan with parchment paper. Make the *pasta frolla* following the directions on page 15. Roll out on a floured surface so that it can fit into the bottom and up the sides of the pan. Set aside. In a bowl, combine the plums with ½ cup of the sugar. Toss them and spoon into the crust. Beat the eggs with the remaining ½ cup of the sugar and the almond extract. Stir in the flour and baking powder and mix until goopy. Drizzle over the plum mixture in the pan. Place in the preheated oven and let bake for 10 minutes, then reduce the heat to 350°F and continue baking for 30 to 40 minutes or until lightly browned on top and set.

Fiadoni di Pasqua - Savory Cheese Turnovers

Makes 50 turnovers

This is a wonderful pastry to serve as an appetizer or to take on a picnic. Although it was traditionally served during Easter, nowadays it is available all year round in the bakeries of *Abruzzo*. It is better to roll the dough with a pasta machine, but if you don't have one, try to roll the dough as thin as possible with a rolling pin.

Pastry dough

2 cups all-purpose flour

¼ teaspoon salt

¼ teaspoon baking powder

1 teaspoon sugar

1 egg

5 tablespoons extra-virgin olive oil

5 tablespoons dry white wine.

Filling

1 ½ pound grams ricotta

12 ounces Parmesan cheese (or a combination of pecorino and Parmesan)

3 eggs

Pinch of nutmeg

Egg wash

1 egg

2 tablespoons water

To make the dough, mix the flour, salt, baking powder and sugar. Add the rest of the ingredients and knead everything together to form an elastic dough. Cover with plastic wrap and refrigerate

for at least 1 hour (or freeze for 20 minutes), or overnight.
To make the filling, drain the ricotta with cheesecloth. Whisk the eggs. Add the remaining ingredients and mix with a wooden spoon until totally blended.
To make the egg wash, mix the egg with the water and set aside.
To assemble the turnovers, roll out a pastry round ⅛-inch thick on a lightly floured surface. With a round, jagged pastry cutter 3 ½-inches in diameter, cut out 6 pastry circles. Place 3 tablespoons of the prepared mixture on each of the circles, leaving a 1/2-inch border. Brush the borders with egg wash. Fold the dough over the filling to form crescent shape. Crimp edges to seal filling inside. Brush the tops with egg wash. Cook the *fiadoni* in the oven heated to 375° F until golden on top and cooked inside. Allow them to cool on a wire rack and then serve at room temperature.

Sweet Tuscan Swiss Chard Crostata

Makes one 10-inch tart

1 *Pasta Frolla* dough recipe (page 15)

2 bunches (1 ¾ pound) chard

½ cup (2.5 ounces) golden raisins

1 cup (5 ounces) blanched almonds, pulverized in food processor

1 ½ cup (1 pound) ricotta cheese strained (or you can substitute small-curd cottage cheese)

1 egg

3 tablespoons sugar

½ teaspoon nutmeg

½ teaspoon salt

Preheat oven to 375°F. Oil and line a 10-inch tart pan with parchment paper. Cover raisins with boiling water and let stand for half an hour. Drain, and chop coarsely. Wash chard well, and remove stalks. Place in large pot, with just the water that clings to the leaves and cook over medium heat for five minutes. Remove, and drain well in colander. Squeeze out as much water as possible. Roll out dough to fill the prepared tart pan and set aside in refrigerator while you finish preparing the filling. In a large bowl shred chard finely and mix with the rest of the filling ingredients until combined. Fill prepared crust and bake for approximately 40 to 45 minutes. Cool on rack. Serve at room temperature.

Focaccia, *Piadina* and other Breads

Sea Salt Focaccia

Makes 1 focaccia

This is the focaccia I use for sandwiches.

1 basic focaccia dough (page 17)

Sea salt

1 half-sheet pan

Make the dough as described in the basic focaccia dough recipe (page 17). After the first rise, oil the pan with oil. Scrape the dough out of the bowl and onto the pan and pat and press the dough into the pan to fill it completely. If the dough resists, wait a few minutes and continue. With a fingertip, make impressions in the dough at 2-inch intervals. Sprinkle sea salt on top of the dough. Cover the dough with plastic wrap and allow the dough to rise again until doubled in bulk (about 45 minutes). Meanwhile, preheat oven to 450 °F and set a rack in the lower third of the oven. When dough has risen, bake until deep golden brown (about 25 minutes).

Gorgonzola, Fig and Prosciutto Focaccia

Makes 1 focaccia

This is my favorite focaccia to serve as an appetizer at the end of a summer meal.

1 basic *focaccia* dough recipe (page 17)

8 oz gorgonzola cheese

3 tablespoon extra-virgin olive oil plus more for the pan

1 pint mission figs, cut in quarters

10 prosciutto slices

½ teaspoon dried thyme

1 half-sheet pan

Mix the gorgonzola and the extra virgin olive oil with a wooden spoon in a mixing bowl. Oil the pan with oil. Scrape the dough out of the bowl and onto the pan and pat and press the dough into the pan to fill it completely. If the dough resists, wait a few minutes and continue. With a fingertip, make impressions in the dough at 2-inch intervals. Drizzle dough with oil. Arrange the gorgonzola mixture and the figs over the top. Allow the dough to rise again until doubled in bulk (about 45 minutes). Meanwhile, preheat oven to 450°F and set a rack in the lower third. When dough has risen, bake until deep golden brown (about 25 minutes). Serve hot with the prosciutto slices over the top.

Potato and Parmesan Focaccia

Makes 1 focaccia

1 basic focaccia dough recipe (page 17)

3 tablespoons extra-virgin olive oil

1 teaspoon sea salt

2 potatoes

¼ cup *Parmigiano-Reggiano*

1 half-sheet pan

Oil the pan with oil. Scrape the dough out of the bowl and onto the pan and pat and press the dough into the pan to fill it completely. If the dough resists, wait a few minutes and continue. With a fingertip, make impressions in the dough at 2-inch intervals. Drizzle dough with oil. Peel and slice the potatoes very thinly and arrange them over the top of the dough covering completely. Drizzle more olive oil on the top and top with parmigiano cheese and salt. Allow the dough to rise again until doubled in bulk, about 45 minutes. Meanwhile, preheat oven to 450 degrees and set a rack in the lower third. When dough has risen, bake until deep golden, about 25 minutes. Check the bottom about halfway through the baking time by lifting the side of the focaccia with a spatula or pancake turner. If it is colouring deeply, slide pan onto another pan to insulate bottom. Slide the focaccia off the pan onto a rack to cool. Serve warm or at room temperature in narrow slices.

Sun Dried Tomato and Feta Focaccia

Makes 1 focaccia

Dough

1 ¾ cup water

1 envelope active dry yeast

2 teaspoons salt

3 ½ cups unbleached, bread flour (King Arthur)

½ cup sun-dried tomatoes

1/4 cup extra-virgin olive oil, plus more for the pan

Topping

1 teaspoon sea salt

½ cup feta cheese

1 half-sheet pan

Warm ⅓ cup of water to 110° F. Dissolve the dry yeast into the water and let it rest for 5 minutes. Add the rest of the water and the flour, and mix until the dough comes together. Add sun dried tomatoes, salt and olive oil and continue kneading until the dough becomes elastic (approximately 15 minutes). Put the dough into a lightly oiled bowl, cover with plastic wrap and allow to rest until it doubles it size (approximately 2 hours). Oil the pan with oil. Scrape the dough out of the bowl and onto the pan and pat and press the dough into the pan to fill it completely. If the dough resists, wait a few minutes and continue. With a fingertip, make impressions in the dough at 2-inch intervals. Drizzle dough generously with oil. Sprinkle with the salt and arrange the feta cheese on the top. Allow the dough to rise again until doubled in bulk (about 45 minutes). Meanwhile, preheat oven to 450 °F and set a rack in the lower third of the oven. When dough has risen, bake until deep golden brown (about 25 minutes). Check the bottom about halfway through the baking time by lifting the side of the focaccia with a spatula or pancake turner. If it is coloring deeply, slide pan onto another pan to insulate bottom. Slide the focaccia off the pan onto a rack to cool.

Sage & Parmesan Focaccia

Makes 1 focaccia

1 basic focaccia dough (page 17)

5 ounces *Parmigiano-Reggiano*, shaved

20 sage leaves

¼ cup extra-virgin olive oil

1 half-sheet pan

Make the dough as described in the basic focaccia dough recipe (page 17). After the first rise, oil the pan with oil. Scrape the dough out of the bowl and onto the pan and pat and press the dough into the pan to fill it completely. If the dough resists, wait a few minutes and continue. With a fingertip, make impressions in the dough at 2-inch intervals. Arrange the filling ingredients over the top. Cover the dough with plastic wrap and allow the dough to rise again until doubled in bulk (about 45 minutes). Meanwhile, preheat oven to 450 °F and set a rack in the lower third of the oven. When dough has risen, bake until deep golden brown (about 25 minutes).

Cheese-stuffed Focaccia

Makes 1 focaccia

1 basic focaccia dough (page 17)

6 ounces mozzarella, sliced

4 ounces Gorgonzola, crumbled

1 handful of basil leaves

½ teaspoon sea salt

2 tablespoon fresh rosemary, chopped

1 half-sheet pan

Make the dough as described in the basic focaccia recipe (page 17). After the first rise, divide the dough in half. Roll out each piece into 9-inch rounds. Place one piece on an oiled baking sheet. Arrange the ingredients over the top, then cover, using the second round crimp edges to seal in the filling. Cover the dough with a piece of plastic wrap and allow the dough to rise again until doubled in bulk (about 45 minutes). Meanwhile, preheat oven to 450 °F and set a rack in the lower third of the oven. When dough has risen, bake until deep golden brown (about 25 minutes).

Pizza Napoli

Makes 2 large pizzas

1 basic pizza dough recipe (page 16)

1 ¼ cup simple tomato sauce (page 18)

¼ cup extra-virgin olive oil, plus more for serving

7 anchovy fillets

1 ½ cups Mozzarella cheese, drained and cut in thin slices

Salt and freshly ground black pepper, to taste

1 tablespoon dried oregano

Position the oven rack in the middle of the oven. If you have a pizza stone, put it on the rack to heat up for 30 minutes. Make the dough as described in the basic pizza dough recipe (page 16). After the first rise, lightly oil two 16-inch pizza pans with olive oil. Preheat the oven to 500°F. On a lightly floured surface, roll and stretch out the ball(s) of dough to an even ¼-inch thickness. Transfer the dough rounds to the prepared pan. Spread the pizza sauce over the crust to the edges. Put cheese on top of the pizza. Put the anchovies on top. Bake until the dough is golden brown and the toppings are very hot, 20-30 minutes for 1 large pizza or 10-12 minutes for individual rounds. Drizzle with the olive oil and season to taste with salt and pepper. Sprinkle with oregano, and serve hot.

Pizza Margherita

Makes 2 large pizzas

1 basic pizza dough recipe (page 16)

1 ¼ cup simple tomato sauce (page 18)

¼ cup extra-virgin olive oil, plus more for serving

1 ½ cups Mozzarella cheese, drained and cut in thin slices

Salt and freshly ground black pepper, to taste

12 basil leaf

Position the oven rack in the middle of the oven. If you have a pizza stone, put it on the rack to heat up for 30 minutes. Make the dough as described in the basic pizza dough recipe (page 16). After the first rise, lightly oil two 16-inch pizza pans. Preheat the oven to 500°F. On a lightly floured surface, roll and stretch out the ball(s) of dough to an even ¼-inch thickness. Transfer the dough rounds to the prepared pan. Spread the pizza sauce over the crust to the edges. Put cheese on top of the pizza. Bake until the dough is golden brown and the toppings are very hot, 20-30 minutes for 1 large pizza or 10-12 minutes for individual rounds. Drizzle with the olive oil and season to taste with salt and pepper. While still hot, arrange the basil leaves on top, cut into wedges, and serve hot.

Schiacciata d'Uva - Flatbread with Raisins and Grapes

Makes 1 focaccia

This flatbread is made in Italy during the fall to celebrate the *Vendemmia* or grape harvest.

1 basic focaccia dough (page 18)

1 cup raisins

6 ounces Vin Santo or another dessert wine

1 pound seedless black grapes

3 tablespoon brown sugar

1 half-sheet pan

Marinate the raisins in the wine for at least two hours or overnight. Make the dough as described in the basic focaccia recipe. After the first rise, oil the jelly roll pan with oil.

Divide the dough in half. Roll out each piece into 9-inch rounds. Place one piece on the oiled baking sheet. Drain the raisins and spread them over the first dough round. Seal in the filling using the second round. Cover the dough with a piece of oiled plastic wrap (oiled side down) and allow the dough to rise again until doubled in bulk, about 30 minutes. Meanwhile, preheat oven to 450 °F and set a rack in the lower third of the oven. Cover the dough evenly with the grapes, lightly pressing them into the dough, and sprinkle the brown sugar on the top. Bake until deep golden brown (about 40 minutes).

Piadina with Prosciutto, Teleme Cheese and Arugula

Makes 5 rounds

Piadina is the most classic bread from the Romagna region (Forlì-Cesena, Ravenna and Rimini) along the Adriatic coast. It is usually made with wheat flour, water, salt and lard (or olive oil) to enrich it and make it flaky and flavorful. *Piadina* is so popular along the Adriatic Coast that there are hundreds of specialized kiosks called *piadinerie* that sell warm *piadinas* filled with a variety of melted cheeses, cold cuts and vegetables. One of the most classic fillings is prosciutto, a creamy cheese like *squaquerone, crescenza or stracchino,* and greens like *rucola* (arugula), but there is also a popular sweet version with fillings such as *Nutella* (chocolate and hazelnut spread) and jam. The variety is limitless! Every family has their own recipe, but there may be small differences depending on the zone of production. *Piadinas* produced around Ravenna are generally thicker, while those produced around Rimini and the Marche region are thinner and of larger diameter.

2 cups all-purpose flour

½ teaspoon baking soda

1 pinch sea salt

2 ounces extra-virgin olive oil

1 cup cold water

10 slices of prosciutto

1 pound *teleme* cheese

1 pound arugula

Combine the flour, baking soda and salt in the bowl of a stand mixer (or in a large bowl if you want to knead it by hand) and mix together. Add the olive oil and the water, just a little bit at a time, and mix on the stand mixer with a dough hook on low speed until the dough starts to form into a ball. Increase the speed to medium, and let it knead until smooth (about 5 minutes). Remove the bowl from the mixer and cover the dough with plastic wrap. Let the dough sit for 30 minutes at room temperature. Heat the griddle on medium-high to quite hot. Divide the dough into 5 pieces, and roll each piece out to 10-inch rounds. The discs should be about ⅛-inch thick. Lightly brush the bread on both sides with olive oil. Place each round on the griddle (depending on the size of your griddle) and cook for about 2 minutes on each side, or until you see little brown spots that mark when it's done. When they are still warm, add the filling ingredients (about 2 oz of cheese, 2 slices of prosciutto, and ½ cup of arugula for each *piadina*)

Piadina with Nutella

Makes 5 rounds

2 cups all-purpose flour

½ teaspoon baking soda

Pinch sea salt

2 ounces extra virgin olive oil (or lard)

1 cup cold water

2 cups *Nutella*

Combine the flour, baking soda and salt in the bowl of a stand mixer (or in a large bowl if you want to knead it by hand) and mix together. Add the olive oil and the water, just a little bit at a time, and mix on the stand mixer with a dough hook on low speed until the dough starts to form into a ball. Increase the speed to medium, and let it knead until smooth (about 5 minutes). Remove the bowl from the mixer and cover the dough with plastic wrap. Let the dough sit for 30 minutes at room temperature. Heat the griddle on medium-high to quite hot. Divide the dough into 5 pieces, and roll each piece out to 10-inch rounds. The discs should be about ⅛-inch thick. Lightly brush the bread on both sides with olive oil. Place each rounds on the griddle (depending on the size of your griddle) and cook for about 2 minutes on each side, or until you see the little brown spots that mark when it's done. When they are still warm, add two tablespoons of nutella on each piadina.

Panzerotti - Fried Calzone with Cheese, Salami and Cherry tomato

Makes 8 to 12 panzerotti

1 basic pizza dough recipe (page 16)

1 cup cherry tomato, cut in half

2 cup ricotta, drained

¼ cup pecorino, grated

¼ cup mozzarella, shredded

½ cup salami, quartered

1 tablespoon extra-virgin olive oil, plus more for frying

8 basil leaves, or to taste, sliced

Sea salt

To make the filling, combine the olive oil, ricotta, pecorino, mozzarella and basil in a mixing bowl.
Divide the dough into 2 ounces or 3 ounces pieces. Roll the pieces into little balls and set them on a lightly floured sheet. Cover with plastic wrap and let rise for ½ hour. Working with a few pieces of dough at a time, roll out each ball on a lightly floured surface to a thin 4-inch round. Place 1 tablespoon of filling on each circle, just to one side of the center. Add tomatoes (one or two), salami, and basil. Lightly brush the edges with water, fold in half to enclose the filling, and seal the edges with a fork. Set each pastry on a rack as it is finished. Repeat with the remaining dough and filling. Let the pastry dry for at least 15 minutes after the last one is completed.

In a deep skillet, heat 1½-inches of oil to 380°F. Working in batches of 4 or 5, carefully slide the pastry into the hot oil and fry until golden on both sides (about 5 minutes). Using a slotted spoon, transfer the tarts to a rack to drain. Serve immediately.

Other Desserts and Pastries

Cannoli Siciliani

Makes 18 cannoli

For this recipe, you will need metal *cannoli* molds.

Stuffing

3 ounces candied lemon peel

3 ounces candied orange peel

¼ cup pistachios

15 ounces ricotta

4 ½ tablespoons powdered sugar

1 teaspoon cinnamon

½ teaspoon salt

1 tablespoon orange-flower water

Cannoli **shell**

2 egg yolks

1 egg

4 tablespoons extra-virgin olive oil

½ cup *Marsala* wine

½ teaspoon salt

2 teaspoons sugar

3 cups flour

Plus;

1 egg, beaten

Olive oil for frying

½ cup confectioners' sugar

For the filling, cut the lemon and orange peels and pistachios very thinly. Drain the ricotta in cheesecloth overnight. Beat the ricotta and sugar until soft. Beat in the rest of the ingredients. Refrigerate for 1 hour, covered with plastic wrap. Meanwhile prepare the shells by mixing the egg yolks, egg, olive oil and *Marsala* in a bowl until combined. In another bowl, mix all the dry ingredients together, then add them to the egg mixture. Mix everything together until it reaches a dough like consistency. Transfer to a lightly floured surface and knead until smooth; the dough will be quite stiff. Chill in plastic wrap for 30 minutes. Lightly dust the work surface with flour and roll the pastry out to 10 x13 inches. Trim the edges, and then cut the pastry into 3-inch squares. Lightly grease the metal cannoli tubes.

Wrap a pastry square diagonally around each tube, securing the overlapping corners with beaten egg and pressing them firmly together. Heat the oil in a deep fat fryer or deep frying pan to 350°F. Fry the shells until golden brown. Place on a plate covered with paper towels. Let the cannoli shells cool, then using a large-tip pastry bag, pipe the ricotta mixture into the cannoli. Lightly dust them with confectioners' sugar before serving .

Chocolate and Olive Oil Mousse

Makes 8 to 10 servings

11 ounces bittersweet (60 percent cacao) chocolate, cut in small pieces

8 large eggs, separated

¾ cup sugar

½ cup extra-virgin olive oil

2 tablespoons brandy

In a double boiler, melt chocolate over low heat. Cool slightly. Beat egg yolks with ½ cup sugar until light. Whisk in olive oil, brandy and melted chocolate.

Using an electric mixer, whisk egg whites until soft peaks form. Add remaining ¼ cup sugar, whisking until stiff but not dry. Fold whites into chocolate mixture so that no white streaks remain. Spoon into an 8 or 10-cup serving bowl or divide among 8 or 10 dessert cups or glasses. Cover with plastic wrap and refrigerate for 24 hours before serving.

Profiteroles

Makes 24 profiteroles

This recipe is wonderful for éclairs and profiterole. I like to serve it with sweetened whipped cream or ice cream. For a dairy free dessert you can use a fruit sorbet instead of the ice cream

⅔ cup all-purpose flour

5 tablespoon extra-virgin olive oil

2 teaspoon granulated sugar

3 eggs

¼ teaspoon salt

Zest of one lemon, freshly grated

⅔ cup water

In a medium sized pot, place the water, salt and oil, and heat until boiling. Add the flour all at ounce, and mix well over the heat for a few minutes, or until the mixture dries and begins to pull away from the pan. This may take anywhere from two to five minutes. Remove from the heat, and pour the paste into a mixing bowl. Beat in the eggs, one at a time. Beat in the sugar and lemon zest. Heat oven to 425 °F. Transfer to piping bag (or mini ice cream scoop) and pipe in desired shapes onto parchment lined baking sheets. Bake until golden and dry (about 20 minutes). To serve them, cut the profiteroles in half and fill them with ice cream, whipped cream or sorbets.

Zeppole - Italian Donuts
Makes 30 zeppole

These small fritters rolled in granulated sugar are very popular during *Carnevale* and you can find them in almost every festival, street fair and holiday in Southern Italy.

⅔ cup water

¼ teaspoon salt

5 tablespoons extra-virgin olive oil

⅔ cup flour

3 eggs

1 tablespoon granulated sugar

Zest of 1 lemon, grated

Oil for deep frying (olive oil or canola oil)

Granulated sugar for topping

Place the water, salt and olive oil in a medium-sized pot and heat until boiling. Add the flour all at once, and mix well over medium heat for a few minutes, or until the mixture dries and begins to pull away from the sides of the pan. This may take anywhere from two to five minutes. Remove from the heat and pour the paste into a mixing bowl to cool it down. Beat in the eggs, one at a time. Beat in the sugar and lemon zest. To fry the *zeppole*, heat the oil to 350°F. Scoop out a spoonful of dough and drop it into the oil. Fry the *zeppole* until golden brown. Drain on a plate covered with paper towels, and then roll them in granulated sugar. Serve them warm.

Amaretto Truffles
Makes 30

8 ounces bittersweet chocolate, chopped

3 ounces extra virgin olive oil

¼ cup amaretto

2 cups *amaretti* cookie crumbs

Melt chocolate in a double boiler. Whisk in olive oil and the amaretto until it is completely melted. Pour into a shallow container, cover, and refrigerate until firm (approximately 3 hours). Scoop out truffles with a melon baller, and roll each truffle into a ball. Chill until firm again. Coat each truffle with the crumbs. Store truffles in the refrigerator in an airtight container.

Homemade Nutella (Chocolate Hazelnut Spread)

This is my version of the traditional Italian chocolate spread that is so popular around the world. This version is healthier and so easy to make. It also tastes much better!

I make it with two of my favorite ingredients: extra virgin olive oil and bittersweet chocolate (70% cacao).

1 pound bittersweet chocolate

1 pound hazelnuts, toasted and chopped

4 ounces extra-virgin olive oil

1 ounce cocoa powder

1 teaspoon vanilla

Chop the chocolate and melt it in a double boiler. Process the hazelnuts and olive oil in a food processor or a blender until you get a nut butter consistency. Sift the cocoa powder and mix it into the hazelnut butter. Add the melted chocolate and the vanilla. Mix everything together. Let it set in the fridge for at least one hour. Serve on bread.

About the Author

Maria Teresa Capdevielle is the author of "My Sweet Abruzzo", a professional pastry chef and a culinary chef/instructor from Abruzzo (Italy). Her local experience includes V-Sattui, The Rose Pistola, The Waterfront, The Market Hall, The Townhouse Grill & Restaurant and a stint at the famed Chez Panisse in Berkeley. She also consults for restaurants and wineries and helps them develop their dessert menu and train their teams.
http://www.mariateresaskitchen.com.

About the Editor

Janet Balsiger is pleased to have been the editor for this unique cookbook. She is currently working as an ESL teacher, while building her freelance copyediting business.
Past collaborations include "Healthy Holidays: A Survival Guide" and "5 Paths to the Love of Your Life: Defining Your Dating Style".

Made in the USA
Middletown, DE
09 July 2015